OXFORD BOOKWORMS LIBRARY
Factfiles

Malala Yousafzai

RACHEL BLADON

Stage 2 (700 headwords)

Series Editor: Rachel Bladon
Founder Factfiles Editor: Christine Lindop

Great Clarendon Street, Oxford, OX2 6DP, United Kingdom

Oxford University Press is a department of the University of Oxford.
It furthers the University's objective of excellence in research, scholarship,
and education by publishing worldwide. Oxford is a registered trade
mark of Oxford University Press in the UK and in certain other countries

© Oxford University Press 2019
The moral rights of the author have been asserted
First published 2019
11

No unauthorized photocopying

All rights reserved. No part of this publication may be reproduced,
stored in a retrieval system, or transmitted, in any form or by any means,
without the prior permission in writing of Oxford University Press, or as
expressly permitted by law, by licence or under terms agreed with the
appropriate reprographics rights organization. Enquiries concerning
reproduction outside the scope of the above should be sent to the ELT
Rights Department, Oxford University Press, at the address above

You must not circulate this work in any other form and you must
impose this same condition on any acquirer

Links to third party websites are provided by Oxford in good faith and
for information only. Oxford disclaims any responsibility for the materials
contained in any third party website referenced in this work

ISBN: 978 0 19 463390 1

A complete recording of this Bookworms edition
of *Malala Yousafzai* is available.

Printed in China

Word count (main text): 8,183

For more information on the Oxford Bookworms Library,
visit www.oup.com/elt/gradedreaders

ACKNOWLEDGEMENTS

Front cover photograph: Richard Stonehouse/Getty Images.

The publisher would like to thank the following for the permission to reproduce photographs:
Alamy Stock Photo pp.4, 52 (Mingora/Shaid Khan), 8, 52 (village/Shadid Khan),
9 (schoolgirls/Xinhua), 11 (street children/Crowdspark), 12 (game of Carrom/Catherine
LeBlond), 17 (Benazir Bhutto/Xinhua), 29 (girls working/Ton Koene), 31 (Mingora street/
Edward North), 43 (Obama/White House Photo), 54 (Nigerian schoolgirls/Picade LLC),
66 (Unicef/ton koene); Eyevine pp.33, 52 (Malala in Peshawar/Polaris); Getty Images
pp.2 (Malala at UN/Andrew Burton), 5 (Pashtun people/Rizwan Tabassum), 16 (Benazir
Bhutto/Derek Hudson), 19, 20 (Malala/Veronquie de Viguerie), 35 (vigil/Asif Hassan),
39 (Malala in hospital/Photo by Queen Elizabeth Hospital Birmingham), 42 (book cover/
AAMIR QUERESHI), 44 (Malal with refugee/AFP), 45 (Nobel Peace Prize/Odd Andersen),
47 (Malala in Pakistan/Abdul Majeed), 55 (Baruani Ndume/AFP); Reuters p.15 (bomb
damage/Faisal Mahmood); Shutterstock pp.iva (Malala/Sipa USA), 3 (Malala family/
Abdulla Sherin), 6 (Malalas father/IBL), 13 (Taliban/Uncredited), 21 (school/Haseeb Ali),
23 (refugees/Greg Baker), 25 (Mingora/Rashid Iqbal), 27, 52 (Lahore/W L NAMKET),
36 (ambulance/Facundo Arrizabalaga), 40 (gifts/p.G.P), 46 (Malala/David Hartley),
48 (Malala/Markus Schrieber), 55 (Mohammed Al Jounde/Robin van Lonkhuisen),
55 (Kehkashen Basu/Jerry Lampen).

Illustrations by: Martin Sanders/Beehive Illustration p.52.

CONTENTS

1	A special birthday	1
2	Family life	3
3	Top of the class	9
4	Changing times	12
5	'I am afraid'	15
6	Escape	22
7	In danger	26
8	'Who is Malala?'	30
9	Fighting to live	32
10	'Where is my father?'	37
11	A new life	41

GLOSSARY	49
REFERENCES	51
MAP OF PAKISTAN	52
TIMELINE	53
THE MALALA FUND	54
THE CHILDREN'S PEACE PRIZE	55
ACTIVITIES: Think ahead	57
ACTIVITIES: Chapter check	58
ACTIVITIES: Focus on vocabulary	63
ACTIVITIES: Focus on language	64
ACTIVITIES: Discussion	65
PROJECT	66
RECOMMENDED READING	68

1　A special birthday

It is 12th July 2013, and at the UN (the United Nations) in New York City, more than six hundred people from many different countries listen quietly to a new speaker. The UN is an important organization which works for peace around the world. It has world leaders and other important people as its speakers all the time, but today, everyone is listening to a sixteen-year-old girl.

The girl's voice is soft and kind – but her words are like fire. She speaks about the children in the world who cannot go to school: the children who have no education because their countries are fighting, or because their families are very poor and they have to work. She asks girls and women to try and make a better world. She calls for peace and love, and education for every child. 'One child, one teacher, one book, and one pen can change the world,'[1] she says.

This girl, who spoke so softly to the world that day – her sixteenth birthday – was Malala Yousafzai. Just nine months earlier, people around the world were shocked when they heard how a gunman got onto her school bus, and shot her in the face. The gunman was from a group called the Taliban, which wanted to stop girls going to school in Malala's home country, Pakistan. He shot Malala because she spoke against the Taliban, at meetings and on the radio, on TV, and online.

Malala at the United Nations, July 2013

But on that day in New York, Malala said to the UN – and to the world – that nothing would stop her trying to get education for everyone. She spent months in hospital after the gunman tried to kill her, but now she felt even stronger than before. 'I am the same Malala,' she said. 'My hopes are the same. And my dreams are the same.'[2]

So, who is Malala Yousafzai? Why does she think that education is so important? And what happened to her after the gunman shot her?

2 Family life

Malala with her mother, father, and brothers

When Malala was born in north-west Pakistan, on 12th July 1997, someone from her father's family came to visit. He brought with him the Yousafzai family tree – a big piece of paper which showed the names of all the important people in Malala's family.

The family tree only had men's names – fathers, brothers, and sons. There were no mothers, sisters, or daughters. But Malala's father Ziauddin wanted everyone to know about his daughter. So he took his pen and wrote 'Malala' under his name.

Even before the Taliban came to north-west Pakistan, the lives of men here were very different from the lives of women. Most people wanted sons, not daughters, so when Malala was born, many of her mother and father's friends were very sorry for them.

But Malala's mother and father were not sorry. They loved their daughter at once, and when people came to visit, Ziauddin asked them to put sweets, money, and fruit into Malala's little bed. People usually only did this when a boy was born, but for Ziauddin and his wife Tor Pekai, their daughter was as important as any boy.

The Yousafzai family lived in Mingora, the biggest town in the Swat Valley, which has beautiful tall mountains all around it. Mingora was five hours by road from Pakistan's most important city, Islamabad, and it was famous for its dancers and singers. In the summer,

Mingora

visitors came from everywhere to watch them and hear their music. It was hot and dry in those summer months: the trees were full of fruit, and there were flowers in the fields and fish in the rivers. But in the winter, Mingora was cold, and the children played in the snow.

The Yousafzais, like many others in the Swat Valley, were Pashtuns – people who have a special history, and who speak a language called Pashto. Ziauddin gave his daughter a very special Pashtun name. He took it from the name of Malalai of Maiwand. She is famous to Pashtun people because when her country's army were fighting, she went to help them, and died.

Pashtun boys

Malala's father loved reading and telling stories about Pashtun history. When he was young, Ziauddin won many competitions for public speaking – making speeches in front of people. When he went to live in Mingora, people soon knew his name because he liked talking about politics, and often spoke at meetings. He was a teacher, and he loved thinking and talking about education, too.

Ziauddin Yousafzai

Three years before Malala was born, Ziauddin opened a school in Mingora called the Khushal School. The school did not do well at first, and when Malala was born, Ziauddin and Tor Pekai were very poor. Like many people in Pakistan, they lived in a small home – two rooms opposite the school, with no kitchen or bathroom – and Malala's mother cooked on a fire on the ground.

Later, the Yousafzais moved to live above the school – and their home was always full of people. Friends and people from their families came to visit, and Ziauddin and Tor Pekai also gave food or a place to stay in their house to poor families who were having a difficult time. They still did not have a lot of money – but they knew that there were many people who were poorer than them.

Family life

For Malala, it was a happy start in life. When she was a little girl, she often walked around her father's school, and she loved standing at the front of the classrooms and talking like a teacher. By the time she was three or four, she went into lessons with much older children, and sat and listened to everything.

Malala soon had two younger brothers, Khushal and Atal, and the three of them played in the streets around their house with other children. They liked playing 'Thief and Police' – but their favourite outside game was cricket, which they played on the roof of their house or in the street.

Malala's father was very busy with his school, or at meetings, so when they were young, Malala and her brothers often did not see him much in the daytime. But in the evenings, when Ziauddin's friends came to drink tea and talk politics, Malala often went and sat at his feet and listened to the conversations.

In the school holidays, the Yousafzais went by bus to visit their family in Shangla, a few hours' drive from Mingora. When the bus left the town behind and went slowly up and up into the hills, Malala always felt excited. Like her father, she loved the beautiful rivers and mountains of Shangla, and she liked to be outside with them around her. When the Yousafzais arrived in their family's village, there was always a big dinner for them: chicken, rice, and vegetables, with plates of apples and sweets, and cups of milky tea.

Malala and her brothers liked playing with their cousins in Shangla. In the mountains, most of the girls

Shangla

did not go to school – and the people from the village thought that Malala was very modern, because she came from a town, liked reading, and wore shoes. But Malala knew that even in Mingora, the life of a Pakistani girl was very different from the life of a boy. When girls got older, they could not go out without a boy or a man. They had to stay inside and cook and do jobs in the house for their brothers and fathers. Malala did not like to think about that. Her mother and father wanted her to feel 'free as a bird'[3] – and she soon knew that she would not be happy with a quiet life at home.

3 Top of the class

After Malala started at the Khushal School, she was soon top of her class. She won many prizes, in school and in the Swat Valley, for her work. Her best friend Moniba was a good student, too, and her work was always more beautiful and tidier than Malala's. But the teachers usually thought that what Malala wrote was better.

Then, when Malala was seven, a new girl called Malka-e-Noor started in her class. In the exams at the end of the year, Malka-e-Noor did better than Malala, and came first. Malala cried and cried: she did not like being second best!

A class at the Khushal School

One day, Malala heard about a public speaking competition at her school. She liked to please her family, and she knew that her father loved public speaking when he was a boy, so she decided to try to win the competition. Malala's father wrote a speech for her. But when Malala got up to speak and saw all the people in the room, she felt very afraid, and lost her place in the speech.

Moniba won the competition, and Malala came second, but this time, Malala was not unhappy. She learned something important, too. She decided to write a speech for herself next time, and to learn it – not read it from a piece of paper.

The Khushal School was getting bigger by this time, and there were now three buildings – a school for younger children, a high school for boys, and a high school for girls. Malala's family moved to a bigger house, but Malala was learning how difficult life was for many other children in Pakistan.

Along the street from the Yousafzais' house was a place for people's rubbish. It smelled very bad, and Malala did not like to walk past it, but one day, her mother asked her to take some old food there. When Malala arrived, she saw a girl who was sitting in the rubbish heap. The girl was no older than Malala. She had dirty hair, and she was sorting the rubbish with some boys – putting things like glass in one place and paper in another.

Malala wanted to talk to the children, but she was too shy. So when her father came home, she asked him to go with her. But when he tried to talk to them, they ran away. Malala wanted her father to give the children free places at his school. Ziauddin explained to her that the children sold some of the rubbish to make money for their families. If they come to our school, he told her, they will be even poorer.

Like Malala, her father wanted these children to go to school and have a better life. So he made leaflets about them – pieces of paper with writing and pictures. He took the leaflets and gave them to lots of people at meetings and in many places in Mingora. Malala wrote about the children, too. She wrote about them in a letter to God. In her letter, she said that she wanted to be a better person, and make the world a better place.

Children working in a rubbish heap, Pakistan

4 Changing times

Most people in Pakistan, like Malala's family, were Muslim, and prayed every day. But by 2004, there were more and more Muslim militants in Pakistan. These were people who felt very strongly about how Muslims lived, and thought that they must fight to get what they want. Many of the militants said that Pakistanis were not living good Muslim lives. Also, they did not like the countries of the west, like the US, and wanted to fight against them and the Pakistani government.

By 2007, Malala and her friends began to see people from a militant group called the Taliban all over the Swat Valley. People from the Taliban spoke on the radio every day. They said that everyone must live, and even wash, in a special way, to be good religious people. Men must have long hair and beards, they said, and everyone must pray each day. Women must stay at home at all times, and girls must stop going to school. Music, dancing, films, and even one of the children's favourite games, Carrom, were bad, they said.

Carrom

Malala's father told her and her mother and brothers not to

Changing times

listen to what the Taliban said. But many people in the Swat Valley – like Malala's mother at that time – had no education. So when religious men told them to do things, they listened.

The Taliban wanted to make many changes in Pakistan, they said. They wanted to take money from the rich and give it to the poor. So a lot of people thought that, with the Taliban as their leaders, life would be better.

The Taliban often carried guns, knives, and sticks. They decided what things were 'wrong', and they drove around and looked for people who were doing any of those things. Because they stopped women going out, Mingora was now very quiet. All the town's music and film shops closed, and the Taliban took people's TVs, DVDs, and CDs, and burned them in the streets.

Malala and her brothers were very worried, because they loved their TV. Their father said that they were

Taliban in the Swat Valley

keeping it. But then the Yousafzais heard that the Taliban listened at people's doors. If they heard a TV, they came in and broke it, people said. So the Yousafzais put their TV in a cupboard, and only watched it quietly – and when anyone knocked at the door, they were very afraid.

One afternoon, Malala came home from school and sat down to watch TV. But there was no picture. That day, the Taliban turned off most of the TV in the Swat Valley. Now Malala and her friends and family could only watch government television. There was no music, no TV, and it was difficult to go out or go to school.

The Taliban were more and more dangerous. They wanted to be Pakistan's new leaders, so they attacked or killed people who worked for the police or the government, and anyone who was against them. Mingora was beginning to feel like a prison for Malala and her family, and for everyone who lived there.

5 'I am afraid'

In autumn 2007, helicopters flew over Mingora, and dropped sweets for the children. Everyone was excited: the army were in town, and people thought that they would quickly send the Taliban away. But for the next year and a half, there was fighting between the army and the Taliban every night. For Malala and her brothers, the sound of bombs and shooting was terrible. They were afraid to be alone, and every night, they went and slept in their mother and father's room.

The Taliban bombed bridges, roads, and shops – but their biggest attacks were on schools. They bombed four hundred schools before the end of 2008, so every morning, when Malala walked to the Khushal School,

Taliban bombing

she closed her eyes and prayed before she arrived there. She loved her school, and she did not want the Taliban to bomb it.

In the years before the Taliban came to the Swat Valley, Malala's father often spoke at meetings to ask for things like better hospitals and schools, and good water, for the people of Mingora. But now, he began to speak against the Taliban. Often, he drove to Peshawar and Islamabad to talk to news reporters about the fighting, and to ask the government for more help for the Swat Valley. Malala sometimes went with him to meetings and spoke to the reporters, too. She talked about girls' education, and how important it was.

Malala's father often talked to her about Benazir Bhutto, who was Pakistan's prime minister – or head of

Benazir Bhutto in 1990

government – in the 1980s and 1990s. Benazir Bhutto was now living outside Pakistan, but she wanted to come back and work in politics again. Because Benazir Bhutto was the first woman leader of a Muslim country in modern times, Malala loved hearing about her.

In autumn 2007, Benazir Bhutto came back to Pakistan from the United Kingdom. She was not afraid of the Taliban, and she wanted to stop the fighting and attacks. Benazir Bhutto wanted to bring change to the country, and give Pakistani women better lives – so when she arrived in Pakistan, Malala and her family were very excited. But in December 2007, Benazir Bhutto died in a shooting and bomb attack.

When the Yousafzais heard this, they were very upset. But Malala began thinking. Because Benazir Bhutto was dead, someone new needed to stand up against the Taliban, and help Pakistan's women. Was this a job for her? When she was younger, she always said that she wanted to be a doctor. But now, she thought that perhaps

The streets of Pakistan after Benazir Bhutto's death

she needed to work in politics. So in the next year, 2008, Malala went with her father more and more often to speak to reporters from Pakistani newspapers, TV, and radio about life under the Taliban.

During those difficult years, school was very important to Malala. She was at the high school now, and the work was harder – but she loved the head teacher of the girls' school, Madam Maryam, and she liked seeing her best friend Moniba every day. At school, for a short time, she and the other girls could think about a bigger world, and try to forget the bombs and guns.

But in December 2008, there was the worst possible news for them. The Taliban said that all girls' schools needed to close from 15th January – they wanted to stop education for every girl, young and old. The Taliban were not the leaders of Pakistan, but lots of people listened to them or were afraid of them. Malala was very upset. What would her days be like, she thought, with no school, and no TV or music?

Other people were thinking about questions like that, too, and in January 2009, a friend of Ziauddin's from the BBC (the famous British TV and radio organization) asked him for some help. The BBC had a website in Urdu – the first language of Pakistan – and Ziauddin's friend needed a student to write a diary for this website about life under the Taliban. At first, an older girl from the Khushal School said that she would write the diary, but then her father came to see Ziauddin. It was too dangerous, he said, and he did not want his daughter to do it.

Malala was only eleven, but when she heard this, she

said to her father that she wanted to write the diary herself. Her father was not sure at first – but when they spoke to Malala's mother, Tor Pekai, she said that she wanted Malala to write the diary. Malala needed to tell people what was happening in Mingora, her mother said.

So, from 3rd January 2009, Malala began to speak to a BBC reporter by phone each day, in Urdu. She was shy at first, but she soon began to talk openly, and the reporter wrote down her words and put them on the website. They could not use Malala's real name because it was too dangerous, so the reporter called her Gul Makai, which was the name of a girl in a Pashtun story.

Malala in 2009

Malala at home

The first day of Malala's Urdu diary was called 'I am afraid'. In the diary, she said that she had bad dreams every night now, because of the fighting between the Taliban and the army. She said that only eleven students from her class of twenty-seven were still coming to school. This was because the Taliban did not want girls to go to school, and people were so afraid of them.

Thousands of people in Pakistan and around the world liked to read the BBC Urdu website, so many people soon saw the diary. Other reporters in many different countries put pieces of it in their newspapers and on their websites, too. But the BBC and the Yousafzais did not want anyone to know who Gul Makai was. So when girls from the Khushal School talked about the diary and showed it to Ziauddin, he had to just smile and say, 'It's very good.'[4]

Because of the Gul Makai diary, many reporters wanted to know more about what the Taliban were doing in Pakistan. So a few days before 15th January, when her school had to close, Malala went with her father to Peshawar, to meet two reporters from the *New York Times*. They wanted to make a film about the Khushal School on its last day, because they knew that the Taliban were closing girls' schools – but when they met Malala, they decided to make the film about her.

On the morning of 15th January, the reporters arrived at the Yousafzais' house, and spoke to Malala when she woke up and got ready for her last day at school. 'They cannot stop me,' Malala said to the camera. 'I will get my education. If it is in home, school, or any place.'[5]

When that last school day came to an end, Malala and her friends did not want to leave. They played their favourite games outside, and when they had to say goodbye to their teachers, they cried and cried. They loved their school. 'Will we ever come back here again?' they asked.

The Khushal School

6   Escape

On 15th February 2009, Malala's family were having lunch when they suddenly heard a very loud gunshot. Malala thought that the Taliban were outside their house, and she was very afraid. But her father said that the gunshots were for peace: the Taliban and the army had a peace plan at last, and they said that the fighting would now stop.

Malala and her family were happy and excited. For a while, there was peace – but the Taliban did not go away. Soon, the fighting began again, and Malala's father heard that the Taliban now wanted to attack Islamabad. In one of Malala's last pieces of writing for the Gul Makai diary, in late February, she said that it was the end of her family's hopes for peace. Mingora was even more dangerous than before, and many people started to leave. By April, the Yousafzais knew that they needed to go, too.

So on 5th May, Malala and her brothers began getting ready to leave their family home and go to Shangla with their mother. Ziauddin was staying in Peshawar, more than two hundred kilometres away from Shangla by road, because he wanted to tell reporters what was happening in the Swat Valley.

Before she left, Malala went up onto the roof of the Yousafzais' house and looked at the mountains around

Mingora, and at the streets below. She remembered playing cricket with her brothers, and all her family's happy times there. 'Will I ever see my home again?'[6] she asked herself.

Then Malala went into the house and packed some clothes, and put all her schoolbooks and papers into her bag. Her brothers were crying because they did not want to leave their chickens. But Malala and her family could not take many things with them – even Malala's schoolbooks had to stay at the house, her mother told her.

Around that time, two million Pashtun people left their homes to escape the fighting between the army and the Taliban. So when Malala and her family drove out of Mingora, with some friends who were leaving, too, the roads were full of traffic. It took them two days to get to Shangla, by car and by bus, and they had to walk the last twenty-four kilometres, carrying their things.

People leaving Mingora, May 2009

For six weeks, Malala and her mother and brothers lived with family in Shangla. Malala went to classes with her cousins – but every day, she thought about her school, her home, and her books. She thought about her father, too.

Malala and her family listened to the radio every day, and at last, there was good news. After weeks of fighting, the government said that Mingora was free from the Taliban. Malala's mother spoke to Ziauddin by phone, and he told them to come to Peshawar.

Malala and her mother and brothers were very happy to see Ziauddin again. Before they went back to Mingora, they visited Islamabad together, because an important person from the US government, Richard Holbrooke, was in the city. Ziauddin went to a meeting with him, and brought his family, too – and Malala spoke to Holbrooke. She said that she was twelve years old, and she asked him to help girls like herself to get an education.

When Malala and her family saw Mingora again, after three months away, they were shocked and upset. The streets were empty, and there were burned cars and dead bodies everywhere. Many of the buildings were now heaps of stone, and there was nothing in any of the shops.

Escape

But their house was fine. The garden was wild, and the chickens were dead – but when Malala ran inside, she found her schoolbooks at once. She and her father went to visit the Khushal School next, and when they saw its walls, they were very happy. There were bullets and rubbish everywhere, and the desks and chairs were in heaps in the corners of the rooms. But that was OK: Malala was home, and she knew that soon she would go back to school.

Mingora, after the Yousafzai family's return

7 In danger

At last, people thought, there was peace in the Swat Valley. The army were still there, but shops opened again, and women could walk freely in the markets once more. On 1st August 2009, the Khushal School opened, and Malala was very excited to see her friends and teachers again.

Over the next few months, Malala spoke at lots of meetings, and early in 2010, she and some other girls from her school went to the District Child Assembly Swat, a political group for children. The group met every month for a year, and they asked Malala to be their speaker. As speaker, she was the leader of the Assembly, and she had to decide who could make speeches.

Under Malala, the Assembly called for help to send street children – very poor boys and girls who live on the streets – to school. They also asked the government to stop young children working, and to build new schools, because the Taliban bombed so many of them.

Malala was busier and busier. In October 2011, she heard that she was a possible winner for a children's peace prize from a group called KidsRights in Amsterdam. Then someone from the government of Punjab, a big place in the east of Pakistan, asked her to speak about education in the important and beautiful old city Lahore. And soon after, she won Pakistan's first peace prize.

Lahore

When Malala went to the prime minister's house in Islamabad to get her prize, she asked him to build new schools for Pakistan, and to open a women's university in the Swat Valley. She was not afraid to talk to politicians. And she knew that one day, she wanted to be a politician, too. She wanted to do things for people, not just ask for help for them.

These were exciting times for Malala – but at home, things were getting more and more difficult. All through 2010 and 2011, there were attacks on people who spoke against the Taliban. And in early 2011, Malala's father got a letter which said that he was in danger. Malala and her family knew now that the Taliban were still in Mingora. After all that fighting, life there was still dangerous.

Then, in January 2012, a Pakistani reporter told Malala's father about something on a Taliban website: the Taliban wanted to kill Malala. Ziauddin was never afraid for himself, and he always thought that because Malala was a child, she was safe. But now, he was very upset. He said that he and Malala needed to stop campaigning for girls' education, and live quietly for a time.

When she was younger, Malala was often afraid of the Taliban – but she was older and stronger now. Her father always said that many things in the world were more important than his life – and she now thought that way, too. 'We can't stop now!'[7] she said.

At first, Malala's father wanted to send her away, to a school outside the Swat Valley. He thought that she would be safer there. But he spoke to one of the Swat army leaders, who said that Malala could stay in Mingora, but needed to campaign in a quieter way. Ziauddin agreed – but he was still very worried about his daughter.

Because 2011 and the beginning of 2012 were so busy for Malala with her campaign work, she did not do very much schoolwork in those months, and in the exams in March, she did not come first. She knew that she needed to spend more time at school.

Another person in Malala's family was now working very hard. Her mother, Tor Pekai, could not read or write at that time. So in spring 2012, she began having lessons with one of the teachers at the Khushal School. She liked learning, and soon she could read in Urdu, and began English lessons, too. Now, in the evenings, Malala and Tor Pekai often sat and did their homework together.

In danger

Malala had her fifteenth birthday that summer, and she thought a lot about what she was doing with her life. She enjoyed talking to people in government, and on the TV and radio, but now she wanted to do something even more important.

She decided to use some of the money from her prizes to start an education foundation – a group to give money to people who need help. Malala often thought about the girl on the rubbish heap. She knew that many girls in her town and in the villages around it did not go to school. Sometimes that was because their families were too poor, so the girls had to work; and sometimes it was because their mothers or fathers did not think that girls needed to have an education.

Malala had a meeting with some girls from her school, and they decided to campaign for a place at school for every girl in the Swat Valley. Malala knew that it was time for her to begin making changes in the world around her.

Girls working in Pakistan

8 'Who is Malala?'

In August 2012, the Taliban attacked one of Ziauddin's best friends, who often spoke against them. He did not die, but Malala saw a change in her father. He walked a different way to school every day now, and looked carefully around before he went inside. And at night, he came into Malala's room and locked her windows.

On Monday 8th October 2012, Malala stayed up late working because she had exams at school. She wanted to come first in the class this time. So on Tuesday 9th, she woke up late.

She quickly had some egg and bread with her tea for breakfast, and then ran out of the house and caught her school bus. She felt happy: she loved school, she enjoyed being with her friends, and she was working hard for her exams. Her exam that day went well, and after school, she and her best friend Moniba decided to take the late bus home because they wanted more time to talk.

Malala and Moniba sat together in the school bus when it came. It was a hot day, and when they drove past the river, it smelled. Ziauddin was always campaigning to stop people putting their rubbish in the Swat River, but it was still dirty, and in the summer, the smell was always terrible.

There were crowds of people in the streets that day, but when the bus turned and drove past a factory, the road

'Who is Malala?' 31

The streets of Mingora

was suddenly very quiet. Then a young man walked out in front of the bus and stopped it. 'Is this the Khushal School bus?'[8] he asked the driver. The young man stood and talked to the driver, and then another man jumped up on the back of the bus, and came in through the door there.

'Who is Malala?'[9] he asked. Malala's school friends turned to look at her, and the man shot Malala in the head three times with a gun.

9 Fighting to live

The men ran away, and Malala fell across Moniba's legs. Blood was coming from her head and ear. When the driver saw this, he went as fast as possible to the hospital, while the Khushal School girls screamed and cried in the back of the bus.

Malala's father Ziauddin was making a speech to four hundred head teachers that afternoon when someone rang him with the news about the shooting. At first, no one said anything about Malala. But when Ziauddin arrived at the hospital, he knew at once that Malala was there, because there were TV cameras and crowds of people outside.

Inside the hospital, he found her: she was lying on a bed with her eyes closed. Ziauddin was shocked and upset. A bullet from the man's gun went into Malala's head, the doctors told Ziauddin, but they said that her brain was not hurt. Now they needed to take her to Peshawar by helicopter, with Ziauddin. The head teacher of the girls' school, Madam Maryam, who was already at the hospital, said that she would go, too.

Malala's mother was still at home, and when people heard about Malala, many women came to the house, crying and praying. One of Ziauddin's friends phoned and said that Malala was going to Peshawar by helicopter, and Tor Pekai needed to follow by car. So when she and

Fighting to live 33

her friends heard the noise of a helicopter, they ran up onto the roof of the building. Pashtun women never took the scarves off their heads – but when the helicopter flew away, Malala's mother took her scarf off and held it up to the sky, praying.

The helicopter soon arrived in Peshawar, and an ambulance took Malala, with Ziauddin and Madam Maryam, to the army hospital. When Colonel Junaid, the doctor there, looked at Malala, he had bad news for Ziauddin. He said that the doctors in Mingora were wrong: her brain was badly hurt, and she was in great danger. That night, after Malala's mother and younger brother Atal arrived at the hospital, Colonel Junaid said that he needed to do an operation.

For five hours, Malala's mother and father waited. Ziauddin was very worried, and Tor Pekai prayed and prayed. Malala was between life and death, and news

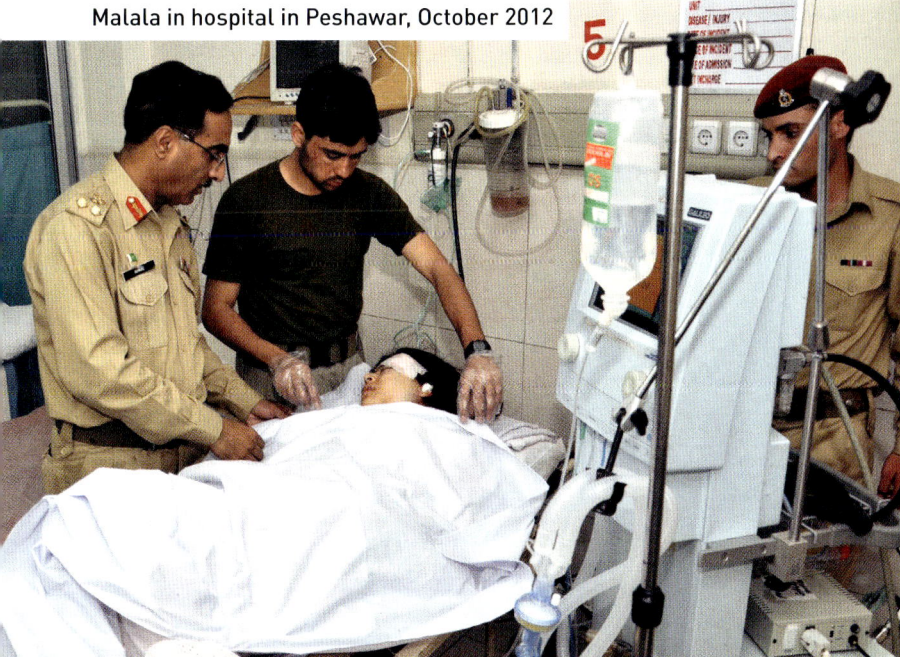

Malala in hospital in Peshawar, October 2012

now came from the Taliban. They shot Malala, they said – not because of her campaign for education, but because she spoke against them and met with leaders from the United States and Europe.

The operation helped Malala, but the doctors now had to put her into a coma (a very deep sleep) to keep her brain safe. Ziauddin already knew that many politicians and people from the government were waiting outside the hospital. But on Wednesday morning, General Kayani, the leader of the army, came to see Malala.

General Kayani knew Malala already, and he was very worried about her. So he spoke to two British doctors who were working with the army in Rawalpindi, two hundred kilometres away, and asked them to come and see her. They arrived by helicopter that afternoon. Malala was out of danger for now, they said – but they thought that she would get worse.

They were right: by Thursday morning, Malala was again fighting for her life. Ziauddin thought that there was no hope for her now. But one of the British doctors, Fiona Reynolds, wanted to take Malala to an army hospital in Rawalpindi. She thought that the hospital there could help her. So Malala and her family went to Rawalpindi in a helicopter.

Because the government and army were so worried about another attack on Malala or her family, there were soldiers all around the hospital in Rawalpindi when they arrived there, and on the roof, too. Only the families of other people in the hospital could come in or out.

There, Dr Reynolds worked with a group of nurses to

Fighting to live

help Malala. At last, Malala was safe, she told Ziauddin after three hours, and she waited while he explained everything carefully to Tor Pekai in Urdu.

People all around the world soon knew about Malala's story, and many countries wanted to help her. Dr Reynolds said that Malala needed to be in a hospital which could help her get better after the shooting and the operations. So on Sunday, the doctors, with the army, decided to move her to the Queen Elizabeth Hospital in Birmingham, in the United Kingdom, which did a lot of work with soldiers who were badly hurt in shootings. But General Kayani had bad news for Ziauddin: because the Yousafzai family did not have the right papers, only Malala's father could travel with her.

Malala's mother and father were very worried about this. They knew that Tor Pekai and her two sons could not stay alone in Pakistan because it was too dangerous.

People in Pakistan pray for Malala

So Ziauddin said to General Kayani that he would not go with Malala. The General and the doctors said that he must, but Ziauddin did not listen. He knew that Malala was safe with Dr Reynolds, he said – and he needed to stay with his family while they waited for their papers to travel together to Birmingham.

On Sunday night, Ziauddin and Tor Pekai came to say goodbye to Malala. Her eyes were closed, and she could not speak – and they were very, very afraid for her. The next morning, the army closed all the roads from the hospital, and put gunmen on every rooftop, and at 5 a.m., an ambulance came to take Malala to the airport. She was flying out of Pakistan, for the first time in her life.

Malala arrives by plane in Birmingham

10 'Where is my father?'

When Malala woke up on 16th October, after a week in a coma, she did not know where she was. She could not see or hear well, and her head hurt terribly. She tried to speak, but she could not say a word, because there was a tube in her neck. Worst of all, she was very worried about her father. When she saw the tubes from her body, she knew that she was in a hospital. But she did not remember the shooting, or know who she was with before it happened. So because her father was not here with her in the hospital, she thought, perhaps he was dead.

Then Dr Reynolds arrived. She spoke to Malala like a friend, but of course Malala did not know who she was. Dr Reynolds gave Malala a present, and Malala wrote in a notebook *Thank you*, and then *Why [do] I have no father?* Then she wrote: *My father has no money. Who will pay for this?*[10]

Dr Reynolds said that Malala's father was safe, and told her not to worry about money. But for those first days, Malala had lots of strange dreams, and sometimes in her dreams, she saw a man with a gun, and her father. She still did not understand why her mother and father were not there, or why she was in hospital.

The doctors, she later learned, did not tell her about the shooting because they did not want her to be shocked and upset. But at last, one day, a doctor came into her room with a mobile phone and said that they were going to call her mother and father. Malala was so happy when she heard her father's voice – but she could not say anything to him because she still could not speak.

After she heard her father on the phone, Malala asked the nurses for a mirror. She looked in it and she saw a face that was now very different. Half of her head had no hair, and on the other half, her hair was very short. Her face was big and round, and black and yellow around her left eye, and the left corner of her mouth went down.

Again and again, Malala wrote in her notebook to ask the nurses and doctors why she was in hospital, and at last, Dr Reynolds told her about the shooting. The bullets hit two other girls in the bus, too, Dr Reynolds told Malala, but they were fine.

At first, Malala could not think about any of this. She only knew that she wanted to go home. But day after day, she began to feel a little stronger. She was very bored in the hospital – but when she began to see better, the nurses brought her a DVD player. On her fifth day in Birmingham, the doctors took the tube out of her neck and she could talk again, so when she spoke to her mother and father the next time, they heard her voice at last.

After ten days in the hospital, Malala was much better, so the nurses moved her to a different room with a window. When she looked out at Birmingham, Malala was not very pleased. The sky was grey, and the houses all looked the same. Where were the mountains? But there was good news for her that day: her mother, father, and brothers were in the United Kingdom at last.

Malala did not cry once in those days when she was in the hospital without her family. But when the door of her hospital room opened, and they came in, she could not stop crying. Her mother and father and brothers were so happy to be with her, but they were shocked when they saw her face. The doctors said that she would need to have many operations. Her face would get better, they said – but it would never be the same again. Before the shooting, Malala always loved to look in the mirror and do her hair, but she was not upset about the changes in her face. She knew that she was lucky to be alive.

Malala's family visited her every day, and she soon knew that they were not the only people who were thinking about her. One day, someone from the hospital brought her a big bag of letters. They were from people all around the world, who wanted her to get better and sent her their love.

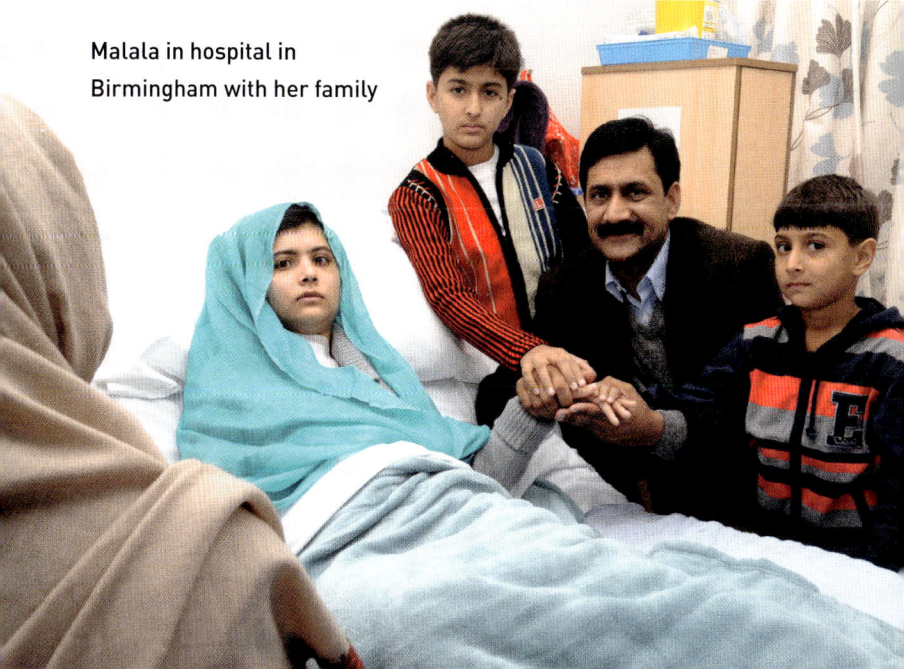

Malala in hospital in Birmingham with her family

Eight thousand letters arrived at the hospital while Malala was staying there, and presents came, too – things like chocolates and flowers, and, best of all, two of Benazir Bhutto's shawls, from her children. World leaders and other famous people wrote to Malala, too – like the film star Angelina Jolie, who she liked very much.

Malala had a big operation on her face, and she had to work hard every day and learn to use her arms and legs again. But slowly, slowly, she got stronger. She remembered things at last, and she began fighting with her brothers again! Malala felt different, too – she was not afraid now, and she said that she had a 'second life'[11]. She knew that she needed to use it to do important things.

Malala in hospital, with presents

11　　　　　　　　　　　　A new life

When Malala came out of hospital in January 2013, three months after the shooting, it was the start of a new life for her and her family. They knew that they could not go back to Pakistan: it was too dangerous. Birmingham was now their new home.

Malala's head did not hurt now, and after more operations, she could hear better and better. Soon, she was ready to start school – and it was a big surprise for her. At her Birmingham school, there were computers and videos in her classrooms, and lessons in things like music. She knew that many children in Pakistan would love to go to a school like her new school, but she wanted to be with her old friends. The girls at her new school were very nice and kind, but to them, she was the girl who nearly died when the Taliban shot her. And she just wanted to be Malala.

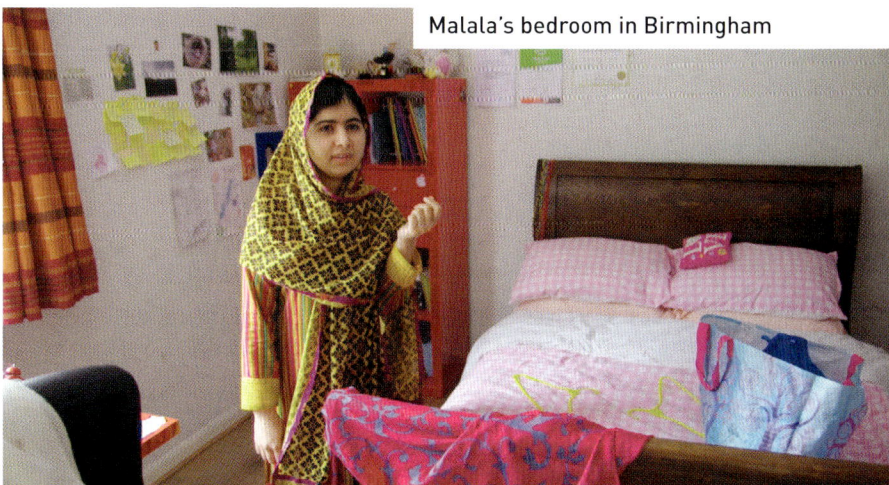

Malala's bedroom in Birmingham

All the Yousafzais wanted to see their friends and family again. They wanted to be in their home town, Mingora, and in the mountains of the Swat Valley – and Malala and her brothers wanted to go back to the Khushal School. Malala spoke to Moniba on her computer for hours, and her mother was always on the phone to her friends and family in Pakistan. Her father had a new job at the UK offices of the Pakistani government, but he thought often of his busy life as a head teacher. The family were happy to be together, and to be safe – but their Birmingham house was quiet and empty, and they remembered their home in Mingora, and the sound of children playing cricket in the streets, and people laughing and talking.

2013 was a very busy year for Malala. With her father, she started the Malala Fund, which campaigns for every child to have an education, and gives money and help to

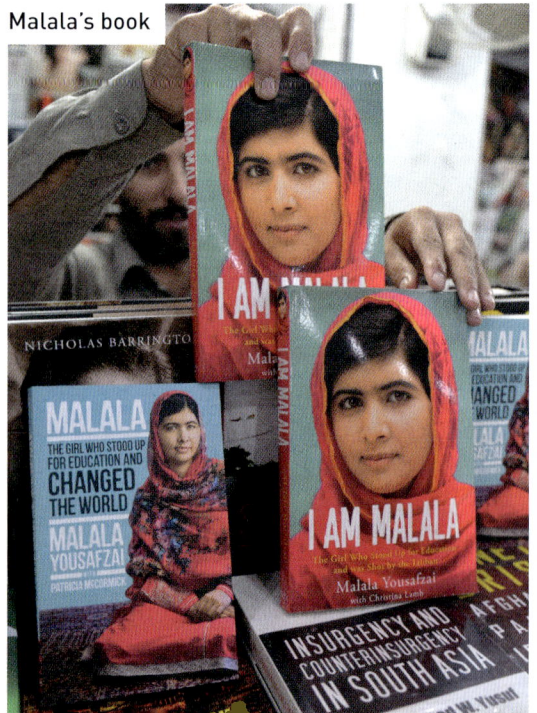

Malala's book

A new life

children and schools all around the world. Malala wrote a book about her life, too, called *I Am Malala*, and in July, she went to New York with her family to give her speech at the United Nations.

Then in October, Malala went to the United States again to meet President Barack Obama, the head of the United States at that time. She talked to him about how important education is, and she told him to use education, not guns, against groups like the Taliban.

Malala found it difficult to make new friends at her school in Birmingham, and often felt shy there, but she was not afraid to speak openly to one of the most important people in the world! When she spoke about education, she was never afraid, because she knew that what she wanted to say was important and that people needed to listen.

With Barack Obama and his family

In February 2014, Malala and her father went to Jordan, to meet people who were leaving Syria because of fighting there. They spoke to families who had no homes, and heard that it was difficult for many children to go to school after they left Syria. So they used money from the Malala Fund to open a school and give lessons to some of the Syrian children who were coming to Jordan and Lebanon.

In that year, Malala was in a lesson at her school in Birmingham when one of her teachers asked her to come out of the class. There was exciting news, her teacher said: she was the winner of the Nobel Peace Prize, a very important prize for people who work for peace in the world. Malala was happy and excited, but she did not leave her lessons to go and talk to the many reporters

In Jordan, with a girl from Syria

Malala wins the Nobel Peace Prize, 2014

who wanted to ask her questions. The prize was for her education campaign, so she thought that it was important for her to finish the school day!

Malala was the youngest ever winner of the Nobel Peace Prize, and there were other big prizes for her in the next few years. She used the prize money to give many children an education – in the Swat Valley in Pakistan, and in different countries around the world.

In 2015, Davis Guggenheim made a film about her life. The film was called *He Named Me Malala*. It talked about how, when Malala was born, her father gave her the name of a famous Pashtun woman in history who was not afraid to put herself in danger to help other people.

Of course, Malala was still at school herself, and she knew that it was important for her to get the best education possible. At school in Birmingham, all her lessons were in English, which was not her first language. But she did well in her exams, and in 2017, she went to Oxford University, one of the best universities in the United Kingdom, as a student.

Malala has not stopped travelling around the world and campaigning for education for all girls with the Malala Fund. In 2016, she visited Dadaab in Kenya, to speak to girls living there who knew that their education was in danger. And in July 2017, she went to Nigeria, which has more girls out of school than any other country in the world.

In March 2018, Malala visited Pakistan again for the first time since the shooting, with her family. She cried

Malala at Oxford University

Malala and her family in Pakistan, March 2018

when she went into her house in Mingora, and said to a family friend that she wants one day to go back to live in Pakistan.

Malala has told her story again in a children's book called *Malala's Magic Pencil*. It is about a special pencil that can bring things to life. But it is also about other, real ways of making changes in the world.

Malala's voice is strong now – and she knows that many people around the world love her and want to help her. When she stood up in front of everyone at the United Nations on her sixteenth birthday, wearing one of Benazir Bhutto's white shawls, she said, 'On 9th October, the Taliban shot me. ... They shot my friends, too. They thought that the bullets would silence us. But ... out of that silence came thousands of voices.'[12] With the help of those voices, Malala knows, she will never stop working to bring education and peace to every child around the world.

Malala speaking about education in 2018

GLOSSARY

attack *(v & n)* to begin fighting or hurting somebody or something

beard *(n)* the hair on a man's face below the mouth

bomb *(n & v)* a thing that explodes (breaks into pieces suddenly), hurting people or breaking things

brain *(n)* Our brain is in our head, and we use it to think and feel.

bullet *(n)* A person puts a bullet in a gun before they shoot it.

campaign *(n & v)* a plan to do things because you want something special to happen

class *(n)* a group of children or students who learn together

competition *(n)* when people do their best at something to try to win

cousin *(n)* the child of your mother or father's brother or sister

cricket *(n)* a game; players try to hit a small, hard ball with a piece of wood (called a bat)

dream *(n)* when you want to do or have something good one day; a picture in your head when you are sleeping

education *(n)* the teaching of somebody at a school or other place

exam *(n)* questions that find out what you know or can do in something, after you have learned it

game *(n)* what you play, like football or tennis

God *(n)* Religious people believe in a god, or gods, that they cannot see.

government *(n)* the group of people who control a country (decide important things about how people there will live)

heap *(n)* a lot of things on top of other things in an untidy way

helicopter *(n)* like a small aeroplane without wings; it flies using a propeller (a thing that turns very quickly)

history *(n)* all the things that happened before now

leader *(n)* a person at the head of a group of people or a country, who controls them (decides what they will do)

meeting *(n)* a time when people meet, usually to talk about something

mirror *(n)* a piece of special glass; you use it to see yourself
Muslim *(n & adj)* a religious person who follows Islam
operation *(n)* when a doctor cuts into somebody's body to take out or look at something inside
organization *(n)* a group of people who do important things together
peace *(n)* when there is no fighting between people or countries
politics *(n)* what people think about how a government needs to control a country; **political** *(adj)*; **politician** *(n)*
pray *(v)* to speak to a god or gods
prize *(n)* what people give to somebody who has done something very well, or who wins something
religious *(adj)* If you are religious, you think that a god or gods (who you cannot see) made the world.
reporter *(n)* a person who writes in a newspaper or speaks on the radio or television about things that have happened
roof *(n)* the top of a building; it goes over your head
rubbish *(n)* When you do not want something, or cannot use it any more, it is rubbish.
safe *(adj)* not in danger
scarf *(n)* Some Muslim women wear a scarf (a long, thin piece of cloth) over their heads.
shawl *(n)* A woman wears a shawl (a big cloth) around the top of her body.
shocked *(adj)* feeling sad, angry, or surprised in a very bad way
shy *(adj)* when it is hard for someone to talk to people they do not know
silence *(v & n)* to stop someone from speaking or making a sound; when there is no sound and everything is quiet
speech *(n)* a talk by someone to a group of people
tube *(n)* a pipe (a long thin piece of plastic, metal, etc. with a hole through it) for moving liquid, e.g. water
university *(n)* Many young people go to university to learn after they have left high school.
upset *(adj)* feeling unhappy or worried

REFERENCES

1. *Malala Yousafzai addresses United Nations Youth Assembly*, 12th July 2013, retrieved September 2018 from https://www.youtube.com/watch?v=3rNhZu3ttIU, 16:36
2. *Malala Yousafzai addresses United Nations Youth Assembly* (12th July 2013), 05:43
3. *I Am Malala: The Girl Who Stood Up for Education and Was Shot by the Taliban*, Malala Yousafzai and Christina Lamb, Weidenfeld and Nicolson, 2014, p.20
4. *I Am Malala: The Girl Who Stood Up for Education and Was Shot by the Taliban* (Yousafzai and Lamb, 2014), p.131
5. *Class Dismissed: The Death of Female Education*, Adam B. Ellick and Irfan Ashraf, 2009, 13:42
6. *I Am Malala: The Girl Who Stood Up for Education and Was Shot by the Taliban* (Yousafzai and Lamb, 2014), p.147
7. *I Am Malala: How One Girl Stood Up for Education and Changed the World*, Malala Yousafzai and Patricia McCormick, Orion, 2015, p.119
8. *I Am Malala: How One Girl Stood Up for Education and Changed the World* (Yousafzai and McCormick, 2015), p.6
9. *I Am Malala: How One Girl Stood Up for Education and Changed the World* (Yousafzai and McCormick, 2015), p.7
10. *I Am Malala: The Girl Who Stood Up for Education and Was Shot by the Taliban* (Yousafzai and Lamb, 2014), p.232
11. *I Am Malala: The Girl Who Stood Up for Education and Was Shot by the Taliban* (Yousafzai and Lamb, 2014), p.261
12. *Malala Yousafzai addresses United Nations Youth Assembly* (12th July 2013), 04:39

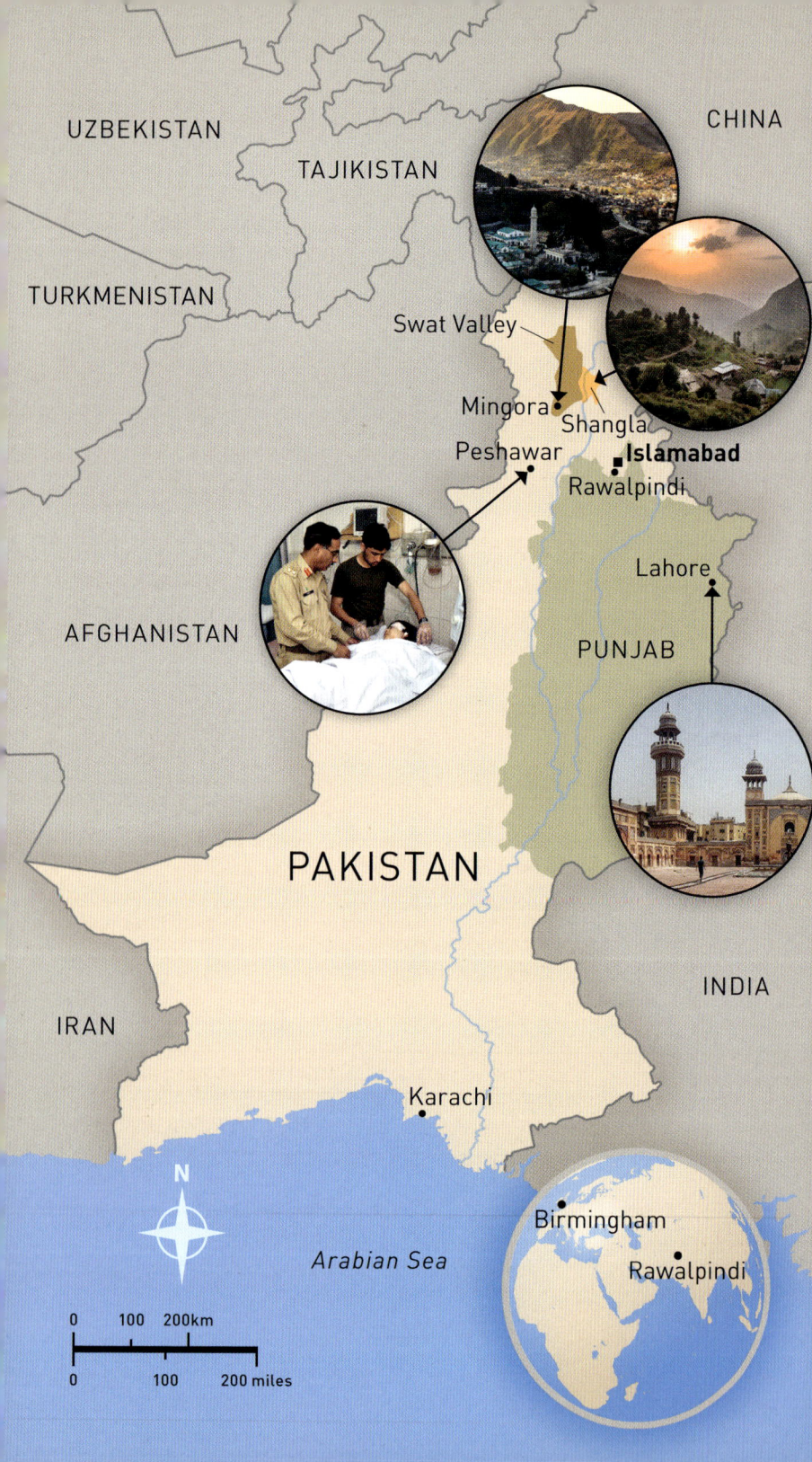

Timeline

1997	• **12th July** Malala is born in Mingora, in the Swat Valley in north-west Pakistan
2007	• Taliban militants take control of the Swat Valley • **December** Militants kill Benazir Bhutto
2009	• **15th January** All girls' schools in the Swat Valley close, because the Taliban want to end girls' education • **January–March** Malala writes the Gul Makai diary for the BBC Urdu website • **May** The Yousafzais, and thousands of other people, leave the Swat Valley, and heavy fighting between the Taliban and the army begins • **July** The Yousafzais come back to Mingora • **August** The Khushal School opens again
2011	• **November** Malala wins a peace prize in Pakistan
2012	• **9th October** A gunman shoots Malala in the head • **15th October** Malala leaves Pakistan in a plane to go to hospital in Birmingham, United Kingdom
2013	• **January** Malala leaves hospital • **March** Malala starts school in Birmingham • Malala writes a book, *I Am Malala* • **July** Malala speaks at the UN in New York City • **October** Malala and her father Ziauddin start the Malala Fund • **October** Malala meets Barack Obama in the United States
2014	• **December** Malala wins the Nobel Peace Prize
2015	• **October** A film about Malala, *He Named Me Malala*, opens in cinemas
2016	• **September** Malala's last day at school: she starts a campaign for education called #YesAllGirls
2017	• Malala writes a children's book, *Malala's Magic Pencil* • **October** Malala begins at Oxford University
2018	• **March** Malala goes back to Pakistan for a visit

The Malala Fund

In 2013, Malala Yousafzai started the Malala Fund with her father, Ziauddin. Around the world, there are more than 130 million girls who are not in school. The Malala Fund campaigns for all girls to have twelve years of free and safe education at a good school.

The Malala Fund works in places that have many girls out of high school. These are countries like Pakistan, India, and Nigeria. The Malala Fund campaigns in lots of different ways:

- It teaches people why some girls cannot go to school – for example, because they are too poor, because they have to work, or because going to school is too dangerous.

- It teaches people why girls' education is important. For example, girls' education makes more jobs for everyone, and brings more money to villages and towns.

- It gives money to help education campaigners around the world. The Malala Fund calls these campaigners 'Gulmakai Champions' (Gul Makai was Malala's name in her diary for the BBC Urdu website). One Gulmakai Champion is Haroon Yasin. He makes videos of lessons for children to watch on their mobile phones if they cannot go to school.

The Children's Peace Prize

KidsRights is an organization which works to help children around the world, and it gives a Children's Peace Prize every year. In 2013, Malala Yousafzai won the prize. Here are some of the other children who won it.

Mohamad Al Jounde (2017)
Together with his family, Mohamad built a school for 200 children who, like him, left Syria because of the fighting and attacks. He began teaching when he was twelve years old, and he takes lots of photos with children because he wants them to learn and enjoy themselves.

Kehkashan Basu (2016)
Kehkashan is from the United Arab Emirates and wants the world to be a greener place. When she was twelve years old, she started a group called Green Hope which planted more than 12,000 trees.

Baruani Ndume (2009)
Baruani left the Democratic Republic of Congo when he was seven because the country was too dangerous. He began living in a camp – a place with hundreds of very small buildings for people who have no home – in Tanzania. At the camp, Baruani started a radio show: he asked children to tell their stories on the radio. Many parents found their lost children because they listened to the show.

Malala Yousafzai

ACTIVITIES

ACTIVITIES

Think ahead

1 Look at the front and back cover. What are you going to read about in this book? Tick (✓) five things.

a famous singer ☐
Malala's life in Pakistan ☐
Malala's sisters ☐
Malala's time in hospital ☐
something terrible that happened to Malala ☐
what Malala is doing now ☐

2 What do you know about Malala Yousafzai? Choose the correct words.

1 Malala was born in *the UK / Pakistan*.
2 Malala was hurt by a *bus / gunman*.
3 She campaigns for girls to go to *school / work*.
4 She was the *youngest / oldest* person to win the Nobel Peace Prize.

3 **RESEARCH** Find out the answers to these questions about Malala Yousafzai.

1 Which books has Malala Yousafzai written?
2 Can you read them in your language?
3 If the answer to question 2 is 'Yes', what are the books' titles in your language?

Chapter check

CHAPTER 1 Which three sentences are true?

1 On 12th July 2013, Malala spoke at the United Nations.
2 Malala spoke about women, peace, and education.
3 Months before she spoke to the UN, someone shot Malala.
4 Malala's dreams changed after a man tried to kill her.

CHAPTER 2 Complete the sentences with the correct names.

Atal   Malala   Mingora   Shangla   Ziauddin

1 The first girl's name on the Yousafzai family tree was _____.
2 The Yousafzai family lived in a beautiful town called _____.
3 Malala's father, _____, was a teacher.
4 Malala liked playing in the school or with her brothers, Khushal and _____.
5 Malala spent the school holidays with her cousins in _____.

ACTIVITIES

CHAPTER 3 Number the sentences in the correct order, 1–5.

a Malala and her father wrote about the poor children.
b Malala came second in a speech competition.
c Malala started going to school.
d Malala cried when she didn't do the best in her exams.
e Malala saw some very poor children at a rubbish heap.

CHAPTER 4 Are these sentences true or false?

1 By 2007, the Taliban were often in the Swat Valley.
2 The Taliban changed the lives of people in the Swat Valley.
3 Everyone in the Swat Valley thought that the Taliban were bad.
4 The Taliban burned the Yousafzais' TV.
5 The Taliban killed people who were against them.

CHAPTER 5 Correct the underlined words.

1 The Taliban's biggest attacks were on <u>bridges</u>.
2 Malala sometimes went to meetings with her father and spoke to <u>the government</u> about girls' education.
3 After Benazir Bhutto died, Malala knew that she wanted to work in <u>hospitals</u>.
4 Malala <u>wrote</u> to a reporter every day to make a diary.
5 In January 2009, reporters from the *New York Times* made a film about Malala's <u>best</u> day at school.

ACTIVITIES

CHAPTER 6 Choose the correct words to complete the sentences.

1 In late February 2009, Mingora became *safer / more dangerous*.
2 When Malala went to Shangla, she put her *clothes / schoolbooks* into a bag, but couldn't take them.
3 In Shangla, Malala heard on the *radio / TV* that Mingora was free from the Taliban.
4 Malala visited Islamabad and met *Barack Obama / Richard Holbrooke*.
5 When Malala went back to Mingora, her house and school were *OK / heaps of stone*.

CHAPTER 7 Number the sentences in the correct order, 1–6.

a Malala visited Islamabad to get Pakistan's peace prize.
b Malala decided to campaign for a place at school for every girl in the Swat Valley.
c The shops and Khushal School opened again.
d Malala and her mother did their homework together.
e Malala became the leader of the District Child Assembly Swat.
f Malala had her fifteenth birthday.

ACTIVITIES

CHAPTER 8 Which three sentences are true?

1 On 8th October 2012, Malala studied hard for her exams.
2 The next day, Malala got ready for school quickly.
3 A man stopped Malala's bus on a busy street.
4 A man got onto Malala's bus and shot her three times.

CHAPTER 9 Complete the sentences with the correct words.

better   brain   bus   Rawalpindi   worse

1 After a man shot Malala, the _____ quickly took her to hospital.
2 In Peshawar, Ziauddin heard that Malala's _____ was badly hurt.
3 Two British doctors visited Malala at the army hospital and said that Malala would get _____.
4 In _____, Dr Reynolds worked to help Malala for many hours.
5 Malala flew out of Pakistan to a hospital in the UK because the doctor thought that she would get _____ there.

CHAPTER 10 Match the sentence halves.

1 When Malala first woke up, …
2 When Malala looked into a mirror, …
3 When Malala saw Birmingham through a window, …
4 When Malala's family came to see her, …
5 When Malala was staying at the hospital, …

a she saw a face that was very different.
b eight thousand letters came for her.
c she was not pleased.
d she could not stop crying.
e she was worried about her father.

CHAPTER 11 Choose the correct answers.

1 Malala left the hospital … after the shooting.
   a three days   b three weeks   c three months
2 The Yousafzais wanted to be in … , but were happy to be together and safe.
   a New York   b Birmingham   c Mingora
3 Malala's first book was called …
   a *I am Malala*.   b *He Named Me Malala*.
   c *Malala's Magic Pencil*.
4 When Malala met Barack Obama, she …
   a felt afraid.   b did not talk to him.
   c spoke about education.
5 Malala went to university in …
   a Pakistan.   b the United Kingdom.
   c the United States.

Focus on vocabulary

1 Complete the sentences with the correct words.

   brain   dreams   mirror   reporter   roof   university

   1 The thing in your head which thinks and learns is your _____.
   2 When students leave high school, some of them go to _____.
   3 A person who writes for a newspaper or is on the TV news is a _____.
   4 You look in a _____ when you want to see yourself.
   5 The thing on top of a house or building is the _____.
   6 When you are sleeping, you sometimes have _____.

2 Find the different word in each group.

   1 exam   scarf   shawl   shoe
   2 bomb   cricket   bullet   gun
   3 shocked   upset   sad   pleased
   4 leader   politician   tube   teacher
   5 helicopter   politics   history   education

Focus on language

1 Complete the sentences with *who* or *which*.

 1 The family tree was a big piece of paper _____ showed the names of people in Malala's family.
 2 The Taliban looked for people _____ watched TV.
 3 Mingora is a town in the Swat Valley _____ has beautiful mountains all around it.
 4 The Queen Elizabeth Hospital did a lot of work with soldiers _____ were badly hurt.
 5 Malala moved to a room _____ had a window.

2 DECODE Read the text and <u>underline</u> *said that*. Then tick (✓) what the people said.

The doctors needed to take Malala to Peshawar, with Ziauddin. Madam Maryam said that she would go, too. One of Ziauddin's friends phoned Malala's mother and said that Malala was going to Peshawar by helicopter, and Tor Pekai needed to follow by car.

 1 a ☐ Madam Maryam said, 'I would go, too'.
   b ☐ Madam Maryam said, 'I'll go, too'.
 2 a ☐ Ziauddin's friend said, 'Malala was going to Peshawar by helicopter.'
   b ☐ Ziauddin's friend said, 'Malala is going to Peshawar by helicopter.'
 3 a ☐ Ziauddin's friend said, 'Tor Pekai needs to follow by car.'
   b ☐ Ziauddin's friend said, 'Tor Pekai needed to follow by car.'

Discussion

1 Read the dialogue. Why does each person think that reading Malala's story is important?

AKAKO: I think that reading Malala's story is important because I learned about life in the Swat Valley and in Pakistan. How about you, Lucas?

LUCAS: After I read Malala's story, I gave some money to Malala's campaign. I think that the story is important because it helps the Malala Fund to get money for its campaigns.

AKAKO: What's your opinion, Mia?

MIA: I think that Malala's story is important because I learned why some girls can't go to school. When I read about her, I understood the lives of lots of girls.

AKAKO: What do you think, Ryan?

RYAN: Well, after I read the story, I thought that I'm very lucky to have an education. I work harder at university now because I read the book.

2 Look at the dialogue again. Underline the three questions Akako asks to find out other opinions.

3 **THINK CRITICALLY** What do you think is the most important reason to read Malala's story?

4 **COMMUNICATE** Discuss your answers to exercise 3 in a group. Use the questions from exercise 2.

PROJECT

1 Find out about three organizations like the Malala Fund which want to change the world. What are their names? Why is their work important?

2 Read this text about UNICEF. Which work that UNICEF does is like the work of the Malala Fund?

> The United Nations Children's Fund (UNICEF) wants the world to be safe for all children. UNICEF works in more than 190 countries and helps children in many ways. For example, it gave food, clean water, and education to many children who left Syria because of fighting. In 2016, UNICEF gave schoolbooks to 15.7 million children around the world.
>
> UNICEF's work is important because, for many children, the world is a dangerous place. Every day, children have to leave their homes because of fighting. Other children do not have food, cannot go to hospital or see a doctor when they are ill, or do not have an education.
>
> You can help UNICEF in lots of ways – for example, you can give money or campaign with them. To learn more about UNICEF, you can visit their website.

3 Read the text again and answer the questions.

   1 What is the organization's name, and what does it do?
   2 Why is its work important?
   3 How can you help the campaign?

4 CREATE Which organization from exercise 1 would you like to learn more about? Answer the questions in exercise 3 for the organization. Use the answers to write a text.

5 Work in small groups and read your texts. For each text you listen to, answer the questions in exercise 3.

6 COLLABORATE You have £500 to give to one of the organizations. Which organization are you going to give the money to? Why? Choose an organization with your group.

If you liked this Bookworm, why not try...

Muhammad Ali

STAGE 2
Andrea Sarto

Even as a young boy, Muhammad Ali knew that he wanted to do great things in his life, and make changes in the world. By the time he was eighteen, he was an Olympic Champion in boxing, and he went on to be World Champion three times. But Ali's fights were not just in the boxing ring. He fought for other things, too: for peace, for black people's rights, for the sick, and for those in need. This is the story of how he became "The Greatest".

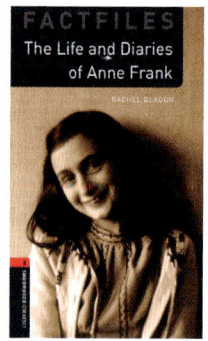

The Life and Diaries of Anne Frank

STAGE 3
Rachel Bladon

From 1942 until 1944, Anne Frank and her family lived secretly in a few rooms at the back of her father's office in Amsterdam, never leaving the building. Like many other Jewish families at that time, they were hiding from Hitler's Nazis.

While she was in hiding, Anne wrote diaries which described her secret life, and the loves, hopes, fears, and dreams of a teenage girl in extraordinary times. After the war, the diaries became famous around the world. This is the story of the diaries of Anne Frank's early years, and of her life during and after the time in hiding.